J 745.5 Bol
Bolte, M.
Eco gifts.
Caledon Public Library
SEP 2015   3582

PRICE: $34.15 (3582/04   )

D1451157

CALEDON PUBLIC LIBRARY

Eco Gifts

UPCYCLED GIFTS
YOU CAN MAKE

by Mari Bolte

CAPSTONE PRESS
a capstone imprint

CALEDON PUBLIC LIBRARY

Snap Books are published by Capstone Press,
1710 Roe Crest Drive, North Mankato, Minnesota 56003
www.capstonepub.com

Copyright © 2016 by Capstone Press, a Capstone
imprint. All rights reserved. No part of this publication
may be reproduced in whole or in part, or stored in a
retrieval system, or transmitted in any form or by any
means, electronic, mechanical, photocopying, recording,
or otherwise, without written permission of the publisher.

Library of Congress Cataloging-in-Publication Data
Bolte, Mari, author.
  Eco gifts : upcycled gifts you can make / by Mari Bolte.
      pages cm. — (Snap books. Make it, gift it)
  Summary: "Step-by-step instructions, tips, and
full-color photographs will help teens and tweens create
personalized presents"—Provided by publisher.
  Audience: Ages 9–12.
  Audience: Grades 4 to 6.
  ISBN 978-1-4914-5202-8 (library binding)
  ISBN 978-1-4914-5218-9 (paperback)
  ISBN 978-1-4914-5218-9 (eBook PDF)

1. Handicraft—Juvenile literature. 2. Gifts—Juvenile
literature. 3. Salvage (Waste, etc.)—Juvenile literature. 4.
Recycling (Waste, etc.)—Juvenile literature. I. Title.

  TT160.B65 2016
  745.5—dc23   2015015947

Designer: Tracy Davies McCabe
Craft Project Creator: Marcy Morin
Photo Stylist: Sarah Schuette
Production Specialist: Laura Manthe

Photo Credits:
All photos by Capstone Press: Karon Dubke

Artistic Effects:
shutterstock

Printed in the United States of America in
North Mankato, Minnesota.
032015   008823CGF15

Table of CONTENTS

Wrap It Up

In a world of craft blogs, activity sites, and pinworthy projects, finding inspiration for personalized gift-giving has never been easier. But where to begin? Find the perfect starting point to create eco-friendly gifts for that special someone in your life.

Here are some simple and eco-friendly wrapping ideas:
- Wrap gifts in pillowcases, tea towels, or scarves. Your guests can use them for years to come.
- Turn cereal, cracker, or juice boxes into gift bags. Cut off the top flaps of the box. Then use a hole punch and pretty ribbon to add handles.
- Repurpose! Use egg cartons to wrap truffles, jewelry, or other small items. Try shredded paper instead of tissue paper in gift bags.

Take A "Bow"

What You'll Need:

newspaper

glue

1. Cut a strip of paper 8 inches (20.3 centimeters) long and ¾ of an inch (2 cm) wide. Repeat until you have eight strips.
2. Fold a strip in half the short way. Then unfold.
3. Twist the ends of each paper strip toward the center, to make a figure-8. Glue the ends to the center. Hold until the ends are set. Repeat with the remaining strips.
4. Stack three of the folded strips on top of each other to create a flower pattern. Glue the strips together.
5. Fold the remaining strips inside the flower. Overlap each strip slightly to create more petals. Let the bow dry completely before use.

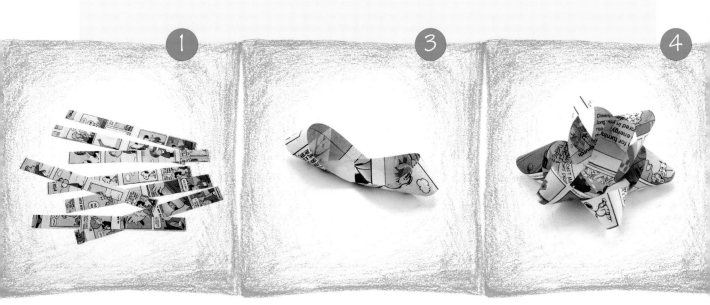

Pretty Pin-Up

This fabric-covered corkboard can be used for a bulletin or organizer board, a jewelry hanger, a set of coasters, or even a small piece of art. Because cork is a sustainable product, it's a great eco gift.

What You'll Need:

iron

three 8-inch (20 cm) squares of fabric

7-inch (18 centimeter) round corkboard

hot glue

ribbon

push pins

1. With an adult's help, iron the fabric to remove any wrinkles.
2. Lay one piece of fabric flat, pattern-side-down. Center the cork on the fabric. Glue the fabric onto the corkboard. Cut off any excess fabric and use glue to tidy up any overlaps.
3. Fold a second square of fabric in half. Iron the fold to make a crisp seam.
4. Lay the folded fabric over half the cork to make a pocket. Glue the fabric to the back of the corkboard. Trim any excess fabric.
5. Repeat step 3 with the third fabric square.
6. Set the folded fabric over a third of the cork to make a pocket. Glue the fabric to the back of the corkboard. Trim any excess fabric and let dry completely.
7. Use glue to add a ribbon loop to the back of the corkboard for easy hanging.
8. Press pins into the corkboard to decorate.

CRAFTING TIPS:

MAKE ONE BIG CORKBOARD OR CREATE SEVERAL SMALLER BOARDS COVERED WITH COORDINATING FABRICS.

DECORATE LARGE FLAT-BACKED TACKS WITH MATCHING FABRIC. TRIM FABRIC PIECES TO THE SAME SIZE OF THE TACK HEADS, AND ATTACH WITH A THIN LAYER OF DECOUPAGE GLUE. ADD A LAYER OF DECOUPAGE GLUE OVER THE TOP OF THE FABRIC TO SEAL.

USE A SINGLE LAYER OF FABRIC TO COVER THE BOARD AND OMIT THE RIBBON FOR A PRETTY TABLE TRIVET.

Fancy Flowers

You've got the gift wrap, but no present! What to do? There's no need to worry when you've got a beautiful bouquet at your fingertips.

What You'll Need:

one 8-10 sheet package of tissue paper

3.5 inch (9 cm) scalloped paper punch

stapler

markers

floral stems and tape

1.5 inch (3.8 cm) wide satin ribbon

corsage pins

1. Unfold the tissue paper. Use the paper punch to cut out a stack of circles and staple each stack in the center.
2. Use markers to color the outer edges of the paper stack, if desired.
3. Begin fluffing the top layer of paper toward the center. Continue until all layers except the bottom layer are fluffed.
4. Fold the bottom layer of tissue paper over a wire stem. Wrap floral tape tightly around the paper and stem.
5. Repeat steps 1–4 until you have enough flowers to make a bouquet.
6. Gather flowers into a bouquet. Wrap the stems tightly with ribbon.
7. For a fancier stem treatment, wrap the ribbon all the way to the bottom of the stems and then back up to the top. Keep the ribbon as flat as possible.
8. Secure the ribbon with corsage pins. Pins should be placed at a downward angle and in a straight line down the entire ribbon wrap.

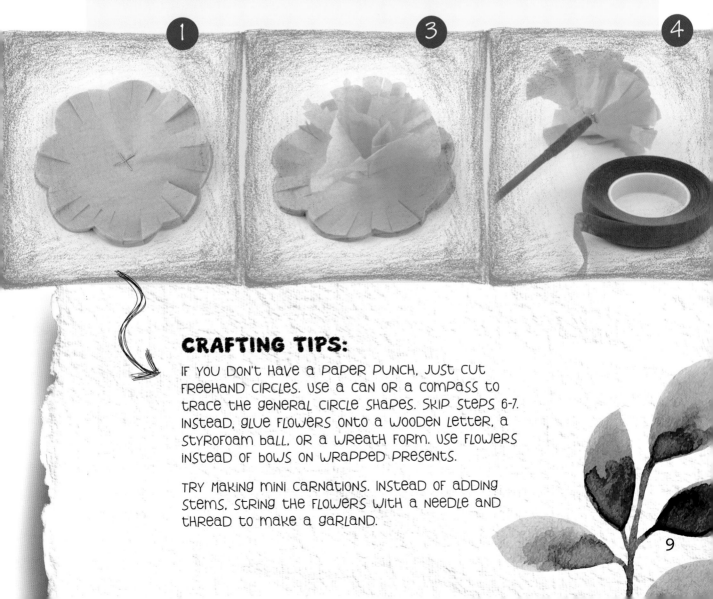

CRAFTING TIPS:

IF YOU DON'T HAVE A PAPER PUNCH, JUST CUT FREEHAND CIRCLES. USE A CAN OR A COMPASS TO TRACE THE GENERAL CIRCLE SHAPES. SKIP STEPS 6-7. INSTEAD, GLUE FLOWERS ONTO A WOODEN LETTER, A STYROFOAM BALL, OR A WREATH FORM. USE FLOWERS INSTEAD OF BOWS ON WRAPPED PRESENTS.

TRY MAKING MINI CARNATIONS. INSTEAD OF ADDING STEMS, STRING THE FLOWERS WITH A NEEDLE AND THREAD TO MAKE A GARLAND.

Labels and Lids

There are many recipes for gifts in a jar. But there's no rule saying the jar can't be as great as the gift that's inside!

What You'll Need:

jar with lid

decorative paper

decoupage glue and paintbrush

masking or painter's tape

chalkboard paint and paintbrush

craft knife

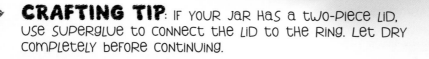

CRAFTING TIP: IF YOUR JAR HAS A TWO-PIECE LID, USE SUPERGLUE TO CONNECT THE LID TO THE RING. LET DRY COMPLETELY BEFORE CONTINUING.

1. Trace the lid onto the plain side of the decorative paper.
2. Cut a circle at least ¼ inch (0.6 cm) larger around than the lid. Snip thin strips all the way around the circle, from the edge of the paper to the edge of your traced circle.
3. Paint a thin layer of decoupage glue onto the top of the lid. Gently press the paper onto the lid, smoothing out any bubbles.
4. Paint a thin layer of decoupage glue onto the inside of the lid. Fold and press the strips along the circle's edge into the glue. Let dry completely. Add another layer of glue over the entire paper-covered area. Let dry completely.
5. Tape off the area of the jar you want to paint. Apply a thin coat of chalkboard paint. Let dry at least 30 minutes. Add additional coats if desired.
6. Remove tape. With an adult's help, use a craft knife to remove any areas where the paint may have scuffed or bled through the tape. Allow paint to cure for at least three days before using for writing.

Here are a few ideas on filling your gift jar:

- cookies, candy, or other sweet selections
- pampering items such as nail polish, lip gloss, and sample-sized sugar scrubs, body butters, and bath bombs
- mixes for treats such as soups, dips, baked goods, or drinks
- a sewing kit with a simple pattern, fabric to make the pattern, and thread, needles, buttons, and pins

11

Puny Plastic

Reuse those plastic containers instead of tossing them! Turn big, bulky pieces of trash into shrunken bits of beauty.

What You'll Need:

measuring tape

clean plastic container

sandpaper

stamp and stamp pad

thin-tipped permanent markers

cookie sheet lined with parchment paper or tinfoil

thin glove or oven mitt

object about the same size as your finger, such as a dowel, marker, spoon handle, nail polish bottle handle, etc.

clear nail polish

1. Use the measuring tape to estimate your ring's finished length and width. Multiply both measurements by 10.
2. Cut a piece from the plastic container that matches your multiplied measurements. Use scissors to round off the corners.
3. Sand one side of the plastic until the surface is rough. Smooth the sharp corners of the plastic with sandpaper.
4. Decorate the sanded side of the plastic with stamps and markers. Colors will concentrate after shrinking, so keep things simple to avoid muddy hues.

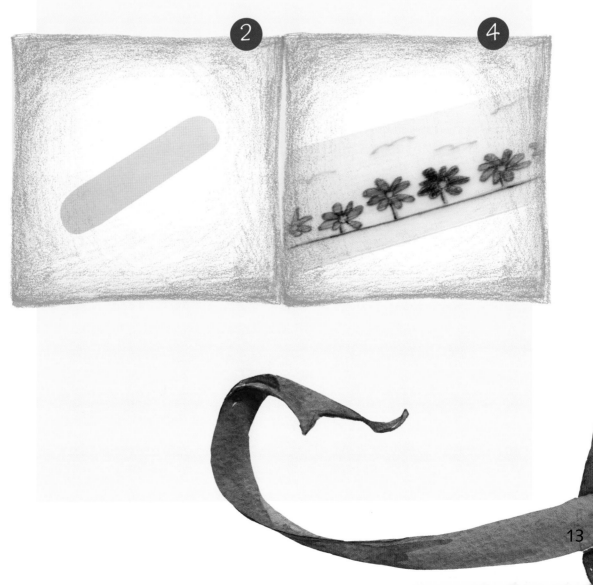

5. Place plastic on cookie sheet. Have an adult place sheet in a 350 degree Fahrenheit (180 degree Celsius) oven for a few minutes. The plastic will curl and then uncurl. When it's flat again, it's ready to come out.

6. Put on the glove or oven mitt to protect your hand. Remove cookie sheet from oven. Working quickly, wrap the plastic strip around the object the same size as your finger. Hold the plastic until it has cooled.

7. Once your ring has cooled completely, coat with a thin layer of clear nail polish to protect your design.

CRAFTING TIP:

USE #6 PLASTIC FOR THIS PROJECT. THE PLASTIC NUMBER CAN USUALLY BE FOUND ON THE BOTTOM OF THE CONTAINER. LOOK FOR CLEAR PLASTIC CLAMSHELL CONTAINERS. USUALLY BAKED GOODS, BERRIES, AND TAKE-OUT MEALS ARE SOLD IN THIS TYPE OF CONTAINER.

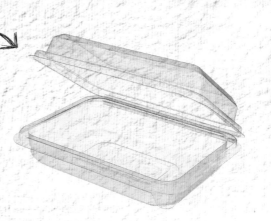

MORE CRAFTING TIPS:

Your plastic may shrink more less than 10 times its size. Some plastics may shrink as little as 3 times their length. Others may shrink more than the 10 times written here. Experiment with different starting lengths of plastic to get the right size ring.

If you don't shape your ring fast enough and it doesn't look just right, don't worry! Have an adult pop it back in the oven with the ring tips in the air. Reheat for about 30 seconds—it should re-flatten. Then try to shape into a ring again.

To give your ring extra dimension, make and shrink flowers or other decorations and glue them onto the ring. But don't stop there—make matching bracelets and necklaces too! Cut the plastic into shapes, and then use a hole punch to make holes before baking. Use jump rings to make a bracelet, or thread onto a chain for a necklace. For a cuff bracelet, follow the ring instructions but start with a much larger piece of plastic. You can find 8 x 10 inch (20.3 x 25.4 cm) sheets online or in craft stores.

Colorful Charge

With a few simple steps, you can create a cute charging station that keeps your electronics in one place and cords tucked safely out of the way.

What You'll Need:

empty soap or shampoo bottle

craft knife

sandpaper

decoupage glue and foam brush

fabric

washi tape

Velcro dots

GIFTING TIP:

FILL THE CHARGING STATION WITH INEXPENSIVE CHARGING CORDS, CELL PHONE COVERS OR SKINS, DUST PLUGS, STYLUSES, EAR BUDS, AND OTHER SMALL ACCESSORIES.

1. Starting at the top of the bottle, cut halfway down the sides. Cut off the front half of the bottle to make a pocket.
2. Trim a square the size of an outlet plug in the back of the bottle.
3. Once you're satisfied with your cuts, sand down all edges until they are even and no longer sharp. Also lightly sandpaper the inside and outside of the bottle.
4. Brush a light coat of decoupage glue onto the outside of the bottle. Press fabric into the glue, wrapping and pressing fabric to avoid bunching and bubbles.
5. Trim any excess fabric. Then add a layer of decoupage glue over everything. Let dry completely.
6. Measure a piece of washi tape 7 inches (20.3 cm) long. Fold the tape in half, sticky sides together. Leave a 0.5 inch (1.3 cm) length from the end unstuck.
7. Flip the tape over and press the sticky end of the tape inside front pocket. The rest of the tape should hang out the front of the bottle.
8. Attach the Velcro to the tape at the top of the front pocket. Stick the other piece of Velcro on the reverse end of the tape. This will create a loop to hold headphones or any excess charge cord.

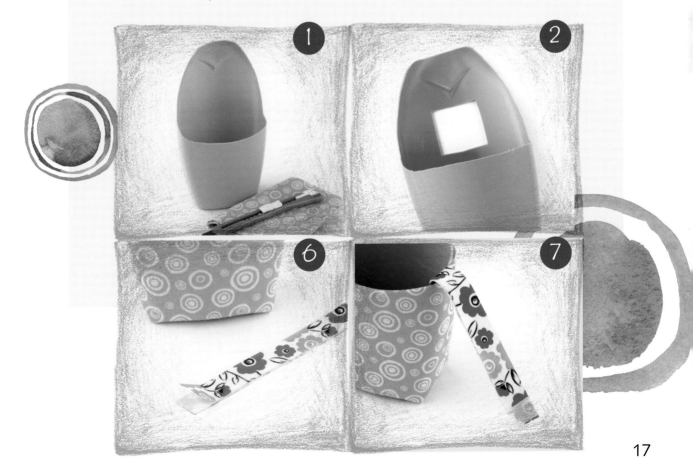

Solid Scents

Solid perfumes are the perfect pocket-sized gift. They can be customized to match your recipient's favorite scents. You can go all natural by using essential oil, or buy fragrance oil. You can also use your favorite bottled perfume.

What You'll Need:

1 tablespoon (15 mL) beeswax

1 tablespoon olive oil

scent, such as essential oil, fragrance oil, or your favorite perfume

old containers, such as lip balm tubes, bottle caps, makeup compacts, or lockets

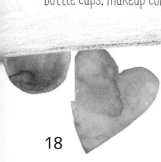

1. If using solid beeswax instead of pellets, grate or chop until the beeswax is in small pieces.
2. Place beeswax and olive oil in a microwave-safe container. Heat for 15 seconds. Then remove from the microwave and stir. Continue heating and stirring until the beeswax is completely melted.
3. Quickly stir in scent. Add until the mixture smells as strong as you'd like. This could be between 20 and 40 drops of essential oil.
4. Pour the mixture into your containers. Let set until solid, between 15 and 30 minutes.

CRAFTING TIPS:

YOU CAN MAKE THIS RECIPE IN ANY QUANTITY. JUST BE SURE TO USE ONE PART BEESWAX TO ONE PART OLIVE OIL.

TO TURN THIS RECIPE INTO A LOTION BAR, ADD ONE PART COCONUT OIL TO THE RECIPE. USE LARGER CONTAINERS, SUCH AS DEODORANT TUBES, PUSH POP CONTAINERS, OR MINT TINS, OR POUR INTO MUFFIN TINS OR SOAP MOLDS.

TO TURN THIS RECIPE INTO LIP BALM, ADD A SQUEEZE OF HONEY. STIR IN A BIT OF LIPSTICK OR EDIBLE GLITTER FOR COLOR, OR A LITTLE POWDERED DRINK MIX FOR COLOR AND FLAVOR. (SKIP THE ESSENTIAL OILS IF YOU USE THE POWDER.)

SOME SUGGESTED ESSENTIAL OILS INCLUDE MINT, CITRUSES SUCH AS LEMON OR ORANGE, LAVENDER, TEA TREE, ROSE, AND VANILLA. TRY COMBINING SCENTS—LEMON AND MINT OR ORANGE AND VANILLA ARE TWO GOOD CHOICES.

Infinity Tee

Nothing says "eco gift" like recycling a well-loved tee. Use a favorite shirt or just pick something in your recipient's color scheme.

What You'll Need:

2 soft T-shirts in different colors; XL or XXL work best

fabric scissors

measuring tape

needle and thread

1. Lay a shirt flat on your work surface. Cut straight across the shirt from armpit to armpit. Discard the top part.
2. Measure 15 inches (38 cm) down from your cut line. Cut straight across. You should have a wide loop of fabric.
3. Fold the loop lengthwise so the cut ends are together. Sew down the whole cut side. Then turn inside out, so your stitches are on the inside.
4. Repeat steps 1-3 with the second shirt.
5. Fold one fabric strip in half and lay flat on your work surface, with the ends facing out. Fold the other fabric strip in half, and face it the opposite direction. Its looped end should overlap the first fabric strip.
6. Slide your hand through the fabric loop on the bottom. Gently pull the ends of the other fabric strip through. You should have a donut-shaped knot.
7. Repeat step 6 as many times as desired. Gently pull the knot tight each time. This should give you a braid with overlapping color layers.
8. Sew the ends of the scarf together.

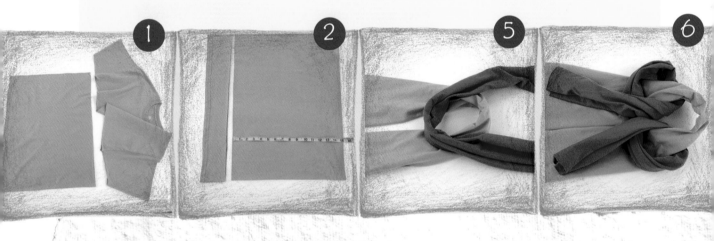

Sewing by Hand:

Slide the thread through the eye of the needle. Tie the end of the thread into a knot. Poke the needle through the underside of the fabric. Pull the thread through the fabric to knotted end. Poke your needle back through the fabric and up again to make a stitch.

Continue weaving the needle in and out of the fabric, making small stitches in a straight line. When you are finished sewing, make a loose stitch. Thread the needle through the loop and pull tight. Cut off remaining thread.

Canine Carry-All

Dog food bags come in a variety of colors and styles. And because they're meant to hold lots of heavy kibble, they can take everyday wear and tear. Upcycle to make the ultimate tote for the dog lover in your life.

What You'll Need:

scissors

clean 30 pound (13.6 kilogram) dog food bag

measuring tape

newspaper

duct tape

clear packing tape

towel

iron

1. Cut along the long side and the bottom of the bag. Open the bag and lay it flat on your work surface.
2. Trim two long strips from the bag, about 20 inches (51 cm) long and 0.75 inch (2 cm) wide. Set the long strips aside to use for handles.
3. Measure and cut out a pattern from the newspaper. The pattern should be 19.5 inches (50 cm) wide and 17.5 inches (44.5 cm) tall. Cut out a 3 inch (7.6 cm) square from the two bottom corners.
4. Trace the pattern onto the dog food bag. Then cut out the pieces. You should have enough space to cut out two pattern pieces.
5. Lay both of the food bag pieces out flat, with the plain sides facing up. Overlap the tabbed edges. This will be the bottom of the bag.
6. Duct tape the tabbed edges together on the inside of the bag. Turn over, and use clear tape on the outside seams.

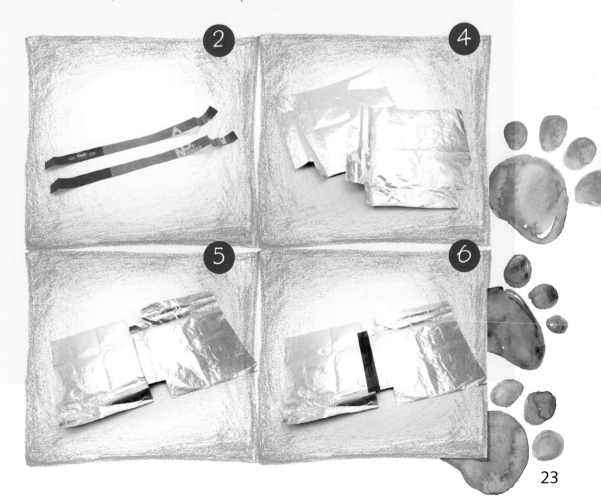

7. Fold the edges together to make the sides of the bag. Repeat step 5, using duct tape on the inside of the bag and clear tape on the outside.

8. Place a towel over the folded edges. With an adult's help, use an iron on low heat over the folds. This will give you nice, crisp creases. The towel will prevent the iron from melting or burning the bag.

9. Once the sides are complete, make a cut about 2 inches (5 cm) long at the top of each corner of the bag. Fold the edges into the bag. Iron the folds, then secure with duct tape.

10. Measure a piece of clear tape, about 21 inches (53 cm) long. Lay it sticky-side-up on your work surface. Center one of the handles you cut in step 2 over the tape. Fold the excess tape over the handle. Repeat so you have two handles.

11. Decide where you want to place the handles. Attach one handle to the bag, leaving the bottom inch (2.5 cm) of both ends uncovered.

12. Fold the bottoms of the handle up over the duct tape. Use more duct tape to press the bottoms to the bag. This will give your handle more stability.

13. Repeat with the second handle.

CRAFTING TIPS:

TO GET RID OF THE DOG FOOD SMELL, RINSE THE BAG WELL WITH DISH SOAP AND LET AIR DRY OVERNIGHT.

DON'T FEEL LIMITED TO DOG. CAT, RABBIT, LIVESTOCK, AND HORSE FEED BAGS ARE OTHER GREAT CHOICES. CAT LITTER, BIRD SEED, AND BULK RICE BAGS WORK WELL TOO.

ASK AROUND TO SEE IF ANYONE HAS BAGS THAT MIGHT WORK BEFORE YOU BUY. IF YOU DO BUY THE BAG BUT DON'T NEED WHAT'S INSIDE, CONSIDER DONATING TO AN ANIMAL RESCUE OR FOOD SHELF.

Books 'n Birds

Treasured tales get a new life with this page-turning birdhouse. Bring a little of your library outdoors with a plain birdhouse and some glue.

What You'll Need:

cardboard

wooden birdhouse

craft knife

hardcover picture book

outdoor decoupage glue and foam brush

1. Make a cardboard template of the front, sides, and back of the birdhouse. Be sure to trace over the entrance hole and perch.
2. Have an adult cut all the pages from the book with a craft knife. Choose which pages you want to use to decorate the birdhouse.
3. Lay the templates over your chosen pages. Trim to fit.
4. Brush a thin layer of decoupage glue over the front of the birdhouse. Carefully press your trimmed book page into the glue. Cover with more decoupage.
5. Repeat with the rest of the birdhouse until all sides are covered.
6. Brush a thin layer of decoupage over the roof of the birdhouse. Set the book cover over the top. Brush the top, sides, and underside of the book thoroughly with decoupage. Let the entire birdhouse dry completely.
7. Add two to three more layers of decoupage, letting each layer dry before adding the next.

CRAFTING TIPS:

IF YOU CAN'T FIND OUTDOOR DECOUPAGE GLUE, USE REGULAR DECOUPAGE GLUE. THEN ADD TWO OR THREE COATS OF A SPRAY SEALANT.

IF YOUR BOOK COVER IS TOO LARGE FOR THE BIRDHOUSE ROOF, TRIM IT INTO STRIPS OR TILES AND OVERLAP THEM LIKE SHINGLES. USE WOOD GLUE TO MAKE SURE THEY STAY ON.

Special Salt Dough

Salt dough is an all-natural, chemical-free way to show you care. Toss a few everyday ingredients together, decorate, and gift! Ornaments, gift tags, and place settings are only a few salt dough ideas.

What You'll Need:

2 cups (480 mL) flour

1 cup (240 mL) salt

1 cup water

rolling pin

parchment paper

large cookie cutter

small cookie cutter

letter stamps and stamp pad

patterned stamps

sandpaper

1. In a large bowl, mix flour and salt. Add water and mix with your hands until the mixture is doughlike.
2. Roll dough out on parchment paper to 0.25 inch (0.6 cm) thick.
3. Use the large cookie cutter to cut out tags.
4. Punch out shapes from the center of each tag with the small cookie cutter.
5. Use letter stamps coated with ink to press your message into the tags. Use patterned stamps for more decoration.
6. Set tags onto a baking sheet lined with parchment paper. With an adult's supervision, bake at 250 degrees F (120 degrees C) for at least 2 hours, or until tags are dry but not browned. The tags are done when they sound hollow when tapped.
7. Gently sand edges until smooth.

GIFTING TIPS:

THIS SALT DOUGH CRAFT IS VERSATILE. TRY THESE VARIATIONS:

* FOR COASTERS, USE A DRINKING GLASS TO CUT OUT DOUGH. SPRAY WITH ACRYLIC SEALER AFTER BAKING TO PROTECT YOUR ART.

* FOR KEYCHAINS, PENDANTS, OR ORNAMENTS, MAKE A HOLE IN THE DOUGH WITH A SKEWER BEFORE BAKING.

* TURN INTO MAGNETS BY ATTACHING STICKY-BACK MAGNETS TO EACH TAG.

* USE LEAVES OR SEASHELLS AS NATURAL STAMPS. COLOR THE INDENTATIONS WITH ACRYLIC PAINT.

* FOR MORE COLOR, KNEAD FOOD COLORING INTO THE DOUGH BEFORE ROLLING.

Hidden Treasures

Candles are a tried and true gift, but what's a person to do with the wax leftover at the end? Don't throw away your old jarred candles. Instead, turn them into the gift that keeps on giving. Toss in a tiny trinket for a fun surprise!

What You'll Need:

large slow cooker

jarred candles in at least three colors: make sure the scents are similar

candle wick

clean candle jar

tinfoil

trinket, such as jewelry, heat-safe toys, or charms

fine glitter

1. Pour several inches of warm water into a large slow cooker. Place jarred candles into slow cooker and heat on high for one hour, or until wax is melted.
2. Dip the metal bottom of the candle wick into some melted wax. Press the wick into the clean candle jar.
3. Fold a double layer of tinfoil around your trinket for protection. Make it as small as possible, and seal the edges well.
4. Carefully pour wax from one jarred candle into the clean candle jar. Use tongs or potholders if the jar is hot. Gently press the trinket into the warm wax.
5. Once the wax has hardened, add another layer of melted wax from another jarred candle. Continue layering until your candle is complete and the trinket is completely covered. Sprinkle glitter over the final layer.
6. Trim wick to 0.5 inch (1.3 cm) long.

CRAFTING TIPS:

IF THE JAR YOU WANT TO USE FOR YOUR NEW CANDLE STILL HAS WAX ON THE BOTTOM, THE FIRST STEP IS TO CLEAN IT OUT! WITH AN ADULT'S' HELP, POUR BOILING WATER INTO THE JARRED CANDLE. THIS WILL SOFTEN THE WAX. USE A BUTTER KNIFE TO GENTLY PRY THE WAX LOOSE. ONCE THE WATER HAS COOLED COMPLETELY, REMOVE THE WAX FROM THE JAR. WASH THE JAR IN WARM, SOAPY WATER.

MAKE SURE YOUR CANDLE SCENTS GO TOGETHER! PAIR ALL HOLIDAY SCENTS OR ALL TROPICAL SCENTS. IF YOU DON'T HAVE ENOUGH OLD WAX TO MAKE A NEW CANDLE, USE PURCHASED WAX TO FILL THE CANDLE JAR.

TO REUSE SMALL AMOUNTS OF WAX, POUR INTO SMALL SILICONE MOLDS OR ICE CUBE TRAYS. YOUR RECIPIENT CAN USE THEM IN CANDLE WARMERS.

Read More:

Jones, Jen. *Planning Perfect Parties: The Girls' Guide to Fun, Fresh, Unforgettable Events.* North Mankato, Minn.: Capstone Press, 2014.

Owen, Ruth. *Gifts.* From Trash to Treasure. New York: PowerKids Press, 2014.

Yasuda, Anita. *Explore Natural Resources!: With 25 Great Projects.* White River Junction. Vt.: Nomad Press, 2014.

Titles in this series: